SECRETS TO CULTIVATE SELF-AWARENESS

DEVELOPING A DEEPER UNDERSTANDING OF YOURSELF

DR. JAGADEESH PILLAI

|| Dedicated to all wisdom seekers around the World ||

॰

Contents

Contents

Prayer

**"Om Bhadram Karnebhih Shrunuyaama
DevaahBhadram Pashyemaakshabhiryajatraah
SthirairangaistushtuvaamsastanoobhihVyashema
Devahitam YadaayuhSwasti Na Indro
VridhashravaahSwasti Nah Pooshaa
VishwavedaahSwasti Nastaarkshyo ArishtanemihSwasti
No Brihaspatir DadhaatuOm Shantih, Shantih, Shantih"**

The literal meaning of this mantra is: OM. O Gods! Let us
hear auspicious words from our ears. O reverent Gods! Let
us behold propitious visions from our eyes, let our organs
and body be stable, healthy, and strong. Let us do that
which is pleasing to the gods in the life span allotted to us.
May Indra, inscribed in the scriptures, bring us fortune!
May Pushan, the knower of the world, grant us prosperity!
May Trakshya, who vanquishes enemies, bestow us with
blessings! May Brihaspati bring us success!
OM Peace, Peace, Peace.

About The Author

Dr. Jagadeesh Pillai is a renowned Guinness World Record holder, writer, and researcher hailing from Varanasi, also known as the abode of Lord Shiva. With a Ph.D. in Vedic Science and a range of creative ideas and achievements, he is a true polymath. He is the author of more than 100 books including Research Publications. Although his roots can be traced back to Kerala, the people of Varanasi hold him in high regard and affectionately consider him one of their own.

In 1998, Dr. Pillai was offered a job at Banaras Hindu University, but he left the position after only two months to pursue greater goals in life. He believed that in order to study Indian scriptures and engage in other creative endeavours, he needed to retire from the daily grind of working solely for money at a young age.

He started an export business from scratch, using the knowledge he had gained from a previous job in the industry. His intelligence and unique approach to business led to great success in a short period of time, earning him more in just a decade and a half than he would have in a lifetime working in a government job. Upon the passing of Dr. APJ Abdul Kalam, Dr. Pillai decided to leave the business and dedicate himself to reading, studying, researching, and experimenting.

During his tenure in the export business, Dr. Pillai traveled to over 16 countries, gaining valuable insight and experiencing the world and life in detail.

Dr. Pillai has achieved four Guinness World Records in the following subjects:

"Script to Screen" - In this record, Dr. Pillai produced and directed an animation film within the shortest time possible, breaking the previous record set by Canadians. He has also received numerous national and international awards and recognitions for this achievement.

Longest Line of Postcards - For this record, Dr. Pillai created a line of 16,300 postcards on the occasion of the 163rd anniversary of Indian Postal Day. The event also included a questionnaire about the Indian flag.

Largest Poster Awareness Campaign - Dr. Pillai designed an awareness campaign on the subject of "Beti Bachao - Beti Padhao" (Save the Girl Child - Educate the Girl Child) to achieve this record.

Largest Envelope - In tribute to the Indian Prime Minister's "Make in India" initiative, Dr. Pillai created a 4000 square meter envelope using waste paper to achieve this record.

Attempted - **70000 Candles on a 210 kg Cake** - To celebrate the 70th Indian Independence Day, Dr. Pillai attempted to light 70,000 candles on a 210 kg cake, which was recorded in World Records India.

Attempted - **Documentary on Dhamek Stupa of Sarnath in 17 Languages** - Dr. Pillai attempted to create a documentary on the Dhamek Stupa of Sarnath, dubbing it in 17 different languages. The result of this attempt is currently awaiting confirmation from the Guinness World Records.

Dr. Pillai is skilled in teaching the Bhagavad Gita, a Hindu scripture, and is popular among young people. He has helped many young people improve their lives through his motivational teachings.

In addition to teaching, he has composed and sung numerous Sanskrit Bhajans and patriotic songs.

He has also written and directed several short films and documentaries for awareness campaigns, and has volunteered with the police in both UP and Kerala to spread awareness about various issues through videos and photography.

Incredibly, he has produced and directed over 100 documentaries about the city of Varanasi, all on his own.

He has also helped and guided more than 25 boys and girls to achieve world records through creative and innovative methods. He is a multifaceted person who uses his intellect and the blessings given to him by God to excel in various areas. He is both a teacher and a student, always learning and teaching, and is able to master any subject he comes across.

He is a selfless social activist and motivational speaker who has overcome struggles and failures to become a successful and enthusiastic individual with a rich life experience.

In addition to his work with the Bhagavad Gita, he is also an efficient Tarot card reader, Astro-Vastu consultant, and a talented singer and composer. He has sung the entire Ram Charita Manas and Bhagavad Gita in his own compositions, and has sung the phrase "Lokah Samastha Sukhino Bhavantu" in 50 different languages. He is currently working on a detailed and scientific study of Vedas, Upanishads, Puranas, and the Bhagavad Gita. He has also composed and sung the Hanuman Chalisa and Gayatri Mantra in 108 and 1008 different compositions, respectively.

Awards - Four Times Guinness World Records, Winner of Mahatma Gandhi Vishwa Shanti Puraskar, Mahatma Gandhi Global Peace Ambassador, Kashi Ratna Award, Dr. APJ Abdul Kalam Motivational Person of the Year 2017, Mother Teresa Award, Indira Gandhi Priyadarshini Award, Bharat Vikas Ratna Award, Udyog Ratna Award, Vigyan Prasar Award, Poorvanchal Ratn Samman.

Preface

This book is designed to help readers cultivate self-awareness and gain a deeper understanding of themselves. It provides a comprehensive look at the various aspects of self-awareness, from understanding one's emotions and motivations to recognizing one's strengths and weaknesses. It also offers practical advice on how to use self-awareness to make positive changes in one's life.

The book is divided into three sections. The first section focuses on understanding the concept of self-awareness and how it can be used to improve one's life. The second section provides readers with practical advice on how to cultivate self-awareness, including tips on how to recognize and manage emotions, set goals, and develop self-confidence. The third section offers readers a variety of exercises and activities to help them further explore their self-awareness.

This book is an invaluable resource for anyone looking to gain a deeper understanding of themselves and make positive changes in their lives. It is written in an accessible and engaging style, making it easy to understand and apply the concepts discussed. With its comprehensive approach to self-awareness, this book is sure to be a valuable asset to anyone looking to gain a better understanding of themselves and make meaningful changes in their lives.

I
Setting the Intention

Setting an intention is a way to focus your energy and attention on the goal you want to achieve. It is a way to create a clear path to success and to ensure that you are taking the necessary steps to reach your desired outcome.

When setting an intention, it is important to be mindful of your thoughts and feelings. Take a few moments to reflect on what you want to accomplish and why. Consider the impact that achieving your goal will have on your life and the lives of those around you. Visualize yourself achieving your goal and the positive changes that will come with it.

Once you have a clear vision of your goal, it is time to create an action plan. Break down your goal into smaller, achievable steps. Make sure to set realistic timelines and to track your progress. This will help you stay motivated and on track.

Finally, it is important to stay focused and to remain open to new ideas and possibilities. As you work towards your goal, be sure to take time to celebrate your successes and to learn from your mistakes. This will help you stay on track and will ensure that you are making progress towards your goal.

By setting an intention and creating an action plan, you can take the first steps towards cultivating self-awareness and developing a deeper understanding of yourself. With dedication and perseverance, you can unlock the secrets to self-discovery and create a life of purpose and fulfillment.

"Self-Awareness is the key to unlocking a deeper understanding of yourself."

&

II

Exploring Your Core Values

Exploring your core values is essential to developing a deeper understanding of yourself. Your core values are the fundamental beliefs that guide your decisions and actions. They are the principles that you live by and the standards you set for yourself. By exploring your core values, you can gain insight into your motivations, desires, and goals.

The first step in exploring your core values is to identify them. Think about what matters most to you and what you believe in. Consider your past experiences and how they have shaped your values. Ask yourself questions such as: What do I stand for? What do I believe in? What do I want to achieve?

Once you have identified your core values, it is important to reflect on them. Ask yourself how your values have impacted your life and how they have shaped your decisions. Consider how your values have changed over time and how they may continue to evolve.

It is also important to consider how your core values align with your goals. Ask yourself if your values are helping you to achieve your goals or if they are holding you back. If your values are not in line with your goals, it may be time to re-evaluate them.

Finally, it is important to take action on your core values. Once you have identified and reflected on your values, it is time to put them into practice. Think about how you can incorporate your values into your daily life. Consider how you can use your values to make decisions and take action.

Exploring your core values is an important part of developing a deeper understanding of yourself. By taking the time to identify, reflect on, and act on your core values, you can gain insight into your motivations, desires, and goals. This can help you to make decisions that are in line with your values and to live a life that is true to yourself.

"The more you know yourself, the more you
can grow."

ॐ

III

Learning to Listen to Your Inner Voice

Learning to listen to your inner voice is an essential part of cultivating self-awareness and developing a deeper understanding of yourself. It can be difficult to tune into your inner voice, especially in a world full of distractions and competing demands. However, with practice and dedication, you can learn to listen to your inner voice and use it to guide you in making decisions and living a more meaningful life.

The first step in learning to listen to your inner voice is to create a quiet space for yourself. This could be a physical space, such as a room in your home, or a mental space, such as a few minutes of meditation. Once you have created a space for yourself, take a few moments to focus on your breath and clear your mind. This will help you to become more aware of your thoughts and feelings.

The next step is to pay attention to your body. Notice any sensations that you are feeling, such as tightness in your chest or a knot in your stomach. These physical sensations can be clues to what your inner voice is trying to tell you.

Once you have become more aware of your body, start to pay attention to your thoughts. Notice any patterns or themes that come up. Your inner voice may be trying to tell you something, so take the time to really listen.

Finally, take action on what your inner voice is telling you. This could be something small, such as taking a break from work, or something bigger, such as making a major life decision. Whatever it is, make sure to trust your inner voice and take action.

Learning to listen to your inner voice is an important part of cultivating self-awareness and developing a deeper understanding of yourself. With practice and dedication, you can learn to tune into your inner voice and use it to guide you in making decisions and living a more meaningful life.

"The journey of self-discovery begins with self-awareness."

೪

IV

Challenging Your Beliefs

As we journey on the path of self-awareness and personal growth, we will inevitably encounter beliefs that limit our potential and hold us back. These beliefs may have been formed in childhood or through experiences that left a lasting impression, but they can also be the result of societal norms and cultural messages that we internalize.

Regardless of their origin, limiting beliefs can have a profound impact on our self-esteem, confidence, and relationships. They can keep us from pursuing our passions and goals, and prevent us from experiencing joy, love, and fulfillment in life.

The good news is that limiting beliefs are not set in stone. With effort and determination, we can challenge and overcome them. In this chapter, we will explore the steps involved in challenging your limiting beliefs, so that you can break free from their hold and cultivate a more positive, empowered perspective.

Step 1: Identifying Your Limiting Beliefs

The first step in challenging your beliefs is to identify them. This can be done by paying attention to your thoughts and feelings, and noticing when you feel stuck or limited. It can also be helpful to write down your beliefs and reflect on how they influence your behavior and attitudes.

Step 2: Questioning the Validity of Your Beliefs

Once you have identified your limiting beliefs, it's time to question their validity. Ask yourself:

Where did this belief come from?

Is it based on facts or assumptions?

Is it consistent with my values and goals?

Does it serve me or hold me back?

By examining your beliefs in this way, you can start to see them for what they are – subjective interpretations of reality – and understand that they can be changed.

Step 3: Replacing Limiting Beliefs with Empowering Ones

The next step is to replace the limiting belief with a more empowering one. This can be done by focusing on the positive aspects of yourself and your life, and reminding yourself that you are capable and worthy of achieving your goals. It can also be helpful to practice self-compassion and to seek out supportive people who encourage your growth and success.

Step 4: Reinforcing the New Belief

Finally, it is important to practice the new belief regularly. This can involve visualization, affirmations, and positive self-talk, as well as surrounding yourself with supportive people and environments. By consistently reinforcing the new belief and making it a part of your everyday life, you can eventually overcome the limiting belief and replace it with a more positive and empowering perspective.

Challenging your limiting beliefs is a process that takes time and effort, but it is well worth it. By breaking free from beliefs that hold you back, you can cultivate a deeper understanding of yourself and unleash your full potential. Remember to be patient with yourself and to practice self-compassion, even when things are difficult. With dedication and perseverance, you will be able to achieve the life you desire.

"The secret to cultivating self-awareness is to
be mindful of your thoughts and feelings."

೩

V

Establishing an Environment of Self-Care

Establishing an environment of self-care is essential for cultivating self-awareness and developing a deeper understanding of oneself. To create a space of self-care, it is important to recognize the importance of taking time for yourself and to prioritize activities that bring joy and relaxation.

One way to begin establishing an environment of self-care is to create a daily routine that includes activities that bring you joy and relaxation. This could include taking a walk in nature, reading a book, listening to music, or engaging in a hobby. Additionally, it is important to set aside time for yourself each day to practice self-care. This could include taking a hot bath, meditating, or journaling.

It is also important to create boundaries with others and to be mindful of how much time you are spending with them. This could include setting limits on how much time you spend with family and friends, or taking time for yourself to recharge. Additionally, it is important to be mindful of how much time you are spending on social media and to limit the amount of time you spend scrolling through your newsfeed.

Finally, it is important to practice self-compassion and to be kind to yourself. This could include speaking to yourself in a positive manner, forgiving yourself for mistakes, and recognizing your own strengths and accomplishments.

By taking the time to create an environment of self-care, you can cultivate self-awareness and develop a deeper understanding of yourself. Establishing a daily routine that includes activities that bring joy and relaxation, setting boundaries with others, and practicing self-compassion are all important steps in creating an environment of self-care. By taking the time to prioritize self-care, you can create a space of peace and relaxation that will help you to cultivate self-awareness and develop a deeper understanding of yourself.

"The more you understand yourself, the more you can appreciate your unique qualities."

৪৩

VI

Embracing the Power of Reflection

Reflection is a powerful tool for cultivating self-awareness and developing a deeper understanding of oneself. It is a process of introspection that allows us to gain insight into our thoughts, feelings, and behaviors. By taking the time to reflect, we can gain a better understanding of our strengths and weaknesses, our motivations, and our values.

Reflection can be a difficult process, as it requires us to be honest with ourselves and confront our own shortcomings. However, it is an essential part of self-growth and development. Through reflection, we can gain a better understanding of our own needs and desires, and how we can best meet them. We can also gain insight into our relationships with others, and how we can better communicate and interact with them.

Reflection can take many forms, from journaling to

meditation. It is important to find a method that works best for you. Journaling is a great way to reflect on your thoughts and feelings, as it allows you to express yourself in a safe and private space. Meditation can also be a powerful tool for reflection, as it allows us to quiet our minds and focus on our innermost thoughts and feelings.

No matter what method you choose, it is important to be mindful and honest with yourself during the process. Reflection can be a difficult and uncomfortable process, but it is essential for self-growth and development. By embracing the power of reflection, we can gain a deeper understanding of ourselves and our relationships with others. This can lead to greater self-awareness and a more fulfilling life.

"The path to self-awareness starts with being
honest with yourself."

&

VII

Identifying Your Strengths and Weaknesses

Self-awareness is an essential part of personal growth and development. Identifying your strengths and weaknesses is a key step in cultivating self-awareness and developing a deeper understanding of yourself.

The first step in identifying your strengths and weaknesses is to take an honest look at yourself. Consider your skills, talents, and abilities, and think about how you can use them to your advantage. Ask yourself questions such as: What do I do well? What do I enjoy doing? What do I find difficult?

Once you have identified your strengths and weaknesses, it is important to focus on developing your strengths and improving your weaknesses. This can be done through self-reflection, goal setting, and taking action.

Self-reflection is an important part of the process. Take time to reflect on your experiences and how they have shaped you. Ask yourself questions such as: What have I learned from my experiences? What have I done well? What could I have done better?

Goal setting is also an important part of the process. Set goals that are realistic and achievable. Think about what you want to achieve and how you can get there.

Finally, take action. Once you have identified your strengths and weaknesses and set goals, it is time to take action. Take small steps towards achieving your goals and focus on the progress you are making.

Identifying your strengths and weaknesses is an important step in cultivating self-awareness and developing a deeper understanding of yourself. Through self-reflection, goal setting, and taking action, you can use your strengths to your advantage and work on improving your weaknesses. With dedication and perseverance, you can become more self-aware and gain a better understanding of yourself.

"The power of self-awareness lies in its
ability to help you make better decisions."

ॐ

VIII
Living Authentically

Living authentically is a key component of cultivating self-awareness and developing a deeper understanding of oneself. To live authentically is to live in alignment with one's true values, beliefs, and desires. It is to be honest with oneself and to live in accordance with one's own truth.

Living authentically requires self-reflection and introspection. It is important to take the time to identify what is truly important to you and to be honest with yourself about your values, beliefs, and desires. This can be done through journaling, meditation, or simply taking the time to sit with yourself and reflect on what matters to you.

Once you have identified what is important to you, it is important to take action to live in accordance with those values. This may mean making changes in your life, such as changing jobs, ending relationships, or taking up a new hobby. It may also mean making small changes, such as setting boundaries with people or taking time for yourself.

Living authentically also requires being mindful of your thoughts and feelings. It is important to be aware of how you are feeling and to take the time to process your emotions. This can be done through journaling, talking to a friend, or engaging in a creative activity.

Finally, living authentically means being kind to yourself. It is important to practice self-compassion and to forgive yourself for mistakes. It is also important to celebrate your successes and to recognize your strengths.

Living authentically is a lifelong journey. It requires self-reflection, taking action, and being mindful of your thoughts and feelings. It also requires being kind to yourself and celebrating your successes. By living authentically, you can cultivate self-awareness and develop a deeper understanding of yourself.

"The key to developing a deeper
understanding of yourself is to be open to
learning new things."

ॐ

IX

The Power of Self-Compassion

Self-compassion is a powerful tool for cultivating self-awareness and developing a deeper understanding of oneself. It is the ability to be kind and understanding to oneself in times of difficulty, rather than being overly critical or judgmental. Self-compassion can help us to recognize our own strengths and weaknesses, and to accept ourselves for who we are.

Self-compassion involves three key components: self-kindness, common humanity, and mindfulness. Self-kindness involves treating oneself with kindness and understanding, rather than with harshness or criticism. Common humanity involves recognizing that all humans experience suffering and difficulty, and that we are not alone in our struggles. Mindfulness involves being aware of our thoughts and feelings without judgment or criticism.

When we practice self-compassion, we are better able to recognize our own strengths and weaknesses, and to accept ourselves for who we are. We can also become more aware of our own needs and feelings, and be better able to respond to them in a healthy way. Self-compassion can also help us to be more understanding and compassionate towards others.

Self-compassion can be cultivated through various practices, such as meditation, journaling, and self-reflection. Meditation can help us to become more mindful of our thoughts and feelings, and to be more accepting of ourselves. Journaling can help us to explore our thoughts and feelings in a safe and non-judgmental way. Self-reflection can help us to gain insight into our own behavior and motivations, and to become more aware of our own needs and feelings.

By cultivating self-compassion, we can become more aware of ourselves and our own needs, and be better able to respond to them in a healthy way. We can also become more understanding and compassionate towards others. Self-compassion can help us to recognize our own strengths and weaknesses, and to accept ourselves for who we are. Ultimately, self-compassion can ead to greater emotional well-being and resilience, improved relationships, and enhanced personal growth and self-improvement. By treating ourselves with kindness and understanding, we can cultivate a positive self-image and a healthy relationship with ourselves, which can improve our overall mental and emotional health.

"Self-awareness is the foundation for
personal growth and development."

ॐ

X
Understanding Your Triggers

Triggers are events, situations, or memories that can cause a person to experience strong emotions, such as anger, fear, or sadness. These triggers can be anything from a traumatic event to a seemingly insignificant comment. It is important to recognize that triggers can be both positive and negative, and that they can vary from person to person.

Once you have identified your triggers, it is important to understand how they affect you. This can be done by reflecting on how you feel when you experience a trigger and how it affects your behavior. It is also important to recognize that triggers can be both conscious and unconscious.

The next step is to learn how to manage your triggers. This can be done by developing coping strategies, such as deep breathing, mindfulness, or journaling. It is also important to practice self-care and to reach out for support when needed.

Finally, it is important to recognize that triggers can be an opportunity for growth. By understanding your triggers, you can gain insight into yourself and your behavior. This can help you to make positive changes in your life and to become more self-aware.

Understanding your triggers is an important part of cultivating self-awareness and developing a deeper understanding of yourself. By recognizing your triggers, learning how they affect you, and developing strategies to manage them, you can gain insight into yourself and make positive changes in your life.

"The best way to cultivate self-awareness is to
take time to reflect on your experiences."

ଚ୍ଚ

XI
Maintaining Healthy Boundaries

Maintaining healthy boundaries is essential for cultivating self-awareness and developing a deeper understanding of oneself. Boundaries are the limits we set for ourselves and others in order to protect our physical, mental, and emotional wellbeing. Establishing and maintaining healthy boundaries is a key component of self-care and can help us to better understand our needs, values, and beliefs.

When it comes to setting boundaries, it is important to be clear and direct. This means communicating your needs and expectations in a straightforward manner. It is also important to be consistent in your boundaries and to be willing to enforce them when necessary. This can help to ensure that your boundaries are respected and that your needs are met.

It is also important to be mindful of the boundaries of others. Respect the boundaries of others and be aware of how your actions may affect them. This can help to foster healthy relationships and create a safe and supportive environment.

In addition to setting and respecting boundaries, it is also important to practice self-compassion. This means being kind and understanding towards yourself and recognizing that mistakes are part of the learning process. Self-compassion can help to reduce feelings of guilt and shame and can help to create a more positive outlook on life.

Finally, it is important to be mindful of your own needs and to take time for yourself. This can help to reduce stress and can help to create a sense of balance in your life. Taking time for yourself can also help to foster self-awareness and can help to create a deeper understanding of yourself.

Maintaining healthy boundaries is an essential part of cultivating self-awareness and developing a deeper understanding of oneself. By setting clear and consistent boundaries, respecting the boundaries of others, practicing self-compassion, and taking time for yourself, you can create a safe and supportive environment and foster a greater understanding of yourself.

"The more you understand yourself, the more
you can accept and embrace your flaws."

ജ

XII

Exploring Limiting Beliefs

Exploring Limiting Beliefs is an essential part of cultivating self-awareness and developing a deeper understanding of oneself. Limiting beliefs are those that hold us back from achieving our goals and living our best lives. They can be deeply rooted in our subconscious and can be difficult to identify and overcome.

Here, we will explore the concept of limiting beliefs and how to identify and challenge them. We will look at the different types of limiting beliefs, how they can manifest in our lives, and how to overcome them.

Limiting beliefs can be defined as any belief that limits our potential or prevents us from achieving our goals. They can be based on our past experiences, our upbringing, or our environment. They can be negative thoughts about ourselves, such as "I'm not good enough" or "I can't do this".

They can also be beliefs about the world, such as "I can't trust anyone" or "I'm not worthy of love".

Limiting beliefs can manifest in many different ways. They can lead to feelings of fear, anxiety, and self-doubt. They can also lead to procrastination, perfectionism, and a lack of motivation.

The first step in overcoming limiting beliefs is to identify them. This can be done by paying attention to your thoughts and feelings and noticing when you feel stuck or limited. Once you have identified your limiting beliefs, you can begin to challenge them. This can be done by questioning the validity of the belief and looking for evidence that contradicts it.

The next step is to replace the limiting belief with a more empowering one. This can be done by focusing on the positive aspects of yourself and your life. It can also be helpful to practice self-compassion and to remind yourself that you are capable and worthy of achieving your goals.

Finally, it is important to practice the new, empowering belief regularly. This can involve visualization, affirmations, and positive self-talk, as well as surrounding yourself with supportive people and environments. By consistently reinforcing the new belief and making it a part of your everyday life, you can eventually overcome the limiting belief and replace it with a more positive and empowering perspective.

It's also important to remember that overcoming limiting beliefs takes time and effort, and that setbacks are a normal part of the process. Be patient with yourself and continue to practice self-compassion and positive self-talk, even when things are difficult. Over time, you will be able to break free from limiting beliefs and achieve the goals and happiness you desire.

"The key to unlocking your potential is to be
aware of your strengths and weaknesses."

છ

XIII

Cultivating Resilience and Adaptability

Cultivating resilience and adaptability is essential for developing a deeper understanding of oneself. Resilience is the ability to bounce back from adversity and adaptability is the capacity to adjust to changing circumstances. Both of these qualities are essential for self-awareness and personal growth.

In order to cultivate resilience and adaptability, it is important to recognize and accept that life is full of challenges and changes. It is important to be open to learning from difficult experiences and to be willing to take risks. It is also important to be mindful of one's thoughts and feelings and to be able to recognize when one is feeling overwhelmed or stuck.

One way to cultivate resilience and adaptability is to practice self-care. This includes taking time for oneself, engaging in activities that bring joy, and setting healthy boundaries. It is also important to practice self-compassion and to be kind to oneself. This can help to build emotional strength and resilience.

Another way to cultivate resilience and adaptability is to develop a growth mindset. This involves believing that one can learn and grow from any situation. It is important to be open to feedback and to be willing to take risks. It is also important to be mindful of one's thoughts and feelings and to be able to recognize when one is feeling overwhelmed or stuck.

Finally, it is important to practice mindfulness. This involves being present in the moment and being aware of one's thoughts and feelings. Mindfulness can help to cultivate resilience and adaptability by allowing one to be more aware of their emotions and to be better able to respond to difficult situations.

Cultivating resilience and adaptability is an essential part of developing a deeper understanding of oneself. By practicing self-care, developing a growth mindset, and practicing mindfulness, one can become more resilient and adaptable. This can help to foster self-awareness and personal growth.

"The secret to cultivating self-awareness is to be mindful of your thoughts, feelings, and actions."

❧

XIV

Reconnecting with Your Passions

Reconnecting with your passions is an essential part of cultivating self-awareness and developing a deeper understanding of yourself. When we become disconnected from our passions, we can feel lost and unfulfilled. Fortunately, there are steps we can take to reconnect with our passions and reignite our enthusiasm for life.

The first step in reconnecting with your passions is to identify what they are. Take some time to reflect on what activities bring you joy and make you feel alive. Think about what you loved to do as a child, what hobbies you have enjoyed in the past, and what activities you have always wanted to try. Once you have identified your passions, make a plan to incorporate them into your life.

The next step is to make time for your passions. This may mean setting aside a few hours each week to pursue your interests or making a commitment to attend a class or workshop. It is important to make your passions a priority and to make sure that you are taking the time to enjoy them.

Another way to reconnect with your passions is to find a community of like-minded people. Joining a club or group related to your interests can be a great way to meet new people and to learn more about your passions. It can also be a great source of motivation and inspiration.

Finally, it is important to be patient with yourself. Reconnecting with your passions can take time and effort, and it is important to be gentle with yourself and to celebrate the small successes.

Reconnecting with your passions can be a powerful and rewarding experience. It can help you to feel more alive and to gain a deeper understanding of yourself. By taking the time to identify your passions, make time for them, and find a supportive community, you can begin to reconnect with the things that bring you joy and fulfillment.

"The journey of self-discovery begins with being honest and open to learning about yourself."

XV

Developing a
Growth Mindset

One of the key factors in cultivating self-awareness and personal growth is developing a growth mindset. A growth mindset is a belief that intelligence, abilities, and personality can be developed through hard work, dedication, and learning from failure. It is the opposite of a fixed mindset, which assumes that traits such as intelligence and talent are set in stone and cannot be changed.

Having a growth mindset can make all the difference in your journey of self-awareness and personal growth. It allows you to approach challenges and failures as opportunities for learning and growth, rather than seeing them as setbacks or proof of your limitations.

Here, we will explore the benefits of developing a growth mindset, and provide practical tips and strategies for cultivating one.

The Benefits of a Growth Mindset

Increased resilience and motivation: People with a growth mindset are more resilient and motivated, because they believe that their efforts and persistence can make a difference in their success and personal growth.

Improved performance and achievement: A growth mindset can lead to better performance and higher achievement, as it motivates you to work harder, seek out new challenges, and learn from your failures.

Greater creativity and innovation: A growth mindset allows you to approach problems and obstacles with a creative and innovative mindset, as you are not limited by fixed beliefs about your abilities.

Enhanced emotional well-being: People with a growth mindset are less likely to experience anxiety, depression, and stress, as they are more resilient in the face of setbacks and more optimistic about their future.

Cultivating a Growth Mindset

Embrace challenges and learning opportunities:

Instead of shying away from challenges, approach them as opportunities for growth and learning. Embrace failure as a necessary part of the process, and view it as feedback for how you can improve.

Celebrate effort and progress:

Focus on the effort you put in, rather than the outcome. Celebrate your progress and acknowledge your hard work, rather than obsessing over your mistakes and shortcomings.

Surround yourself with positive, supportive people:

Seek out people who encourage and support your growth, rather than those who put you down or limit your potential.

Cultivate a positive self-image:

Practice self-compassion and focus on your strengths and positive qualities, rather than dwelling on your weaknesses and limitations.

Embrace new learning experiences:

Stay curious and open to new experiences, and seek out opportunities for learning and growth.

Developing a growth mindset is a crucial step in cultivating self-awareness and personal growth. By embracing challenges and learning opportunities, celebrating effort and progress, and cultivating a positive self-image, you can cultivate a growth mindset that will allow you to reach your full potential and achieve the life you desire. With persistence and dedication, you can overcome limiting beliefs and cultivate a deeper understanding of yourself and your capabilities.

"The power of self-awareness lies in its
ability to help you make informed decisions
and take meaningful action."

ॐ

Other Books Of The Author

1. The Moments When I Met God
2. Kashiyile Theertha Pathangal
3. GURU GYAN VANI
4. Abhiprerak Gita
5. ASSI SE JAIN GHAT TAK
6. Hopelessness of Arjuna
7. The Soul and It's True Nature
8. Sense of Action (Karma)
9. Action through Wisdom
10. Action through Wisdom
11. THEORY AND PRACTICAL OF EVERY ACTION
12. LOGICAL UNDERSTANDING OF THE SUPREME
13. THE IMPERISHABLE SUPREME
14. Yatra Nishadraj se Hanuman Ghat Tak
15. Yatra Karnatak Ghat se Raja Ghat Tak
16. Yatra Pandey Ghat se Prayagraj Ghat Tak
17. Yatra Ranjendra Prasad Ghat se Dattatreya Ghat Tak
18. YaatraSindhiya Ghat se Gwaliar Ghat Tak
19. Yatra Mangala Gauri Ghat se Hanuman Gadhi Ghat Tak
20. Yatra Gaay Ghat Se Nishad Ghat Tak
21. MAA GANGA, GHATEN EVM UTSAV
22. Ganga Arti Dev Deepavali evam Any Utsav
23. Potentials of Digitalized India
24. VEDIC CONSCIOUSNESS
25. A Brief Introduction to Vedic Science
26. Kashi ke Barah Jyotirling
27. IMPACT OF MOTIVATION
28. Let's have a Milky Way Journey
29. Color Therapy in a Nutshell

30. Rigveda in a Nutshell
31. Yajurveda in a Nutshell
32. Samveda in a Nutshell
33. Atharva Veda in a Nutshell
34. Ayushman Bhava - Ayurveda
35. Srimad Bhagavad Gita and Upanishad Connection
36. Srimad Bhagavad Gita - an attempt to summarize each chapter.
37. Facts and Impact of Nakshatra
38. Astro Gems - NAVARATNA
39. Ekadashi - A Concise Overview
40. A Concise View of Hanuman Chalisa
41. Inspirational Gita
42. Nakshatraranyam
43. Summary of 18 Mahapuranas
44. Synopsis of 18 Upa Puranas
45. Rigvediya Upanishads
46. Shukla Yajurvediya Upanishads
47. Krishna Yajurvediya Upanishads
48. Samavediya Upanishads
49. Atharvavediya Upanishads
50. The Seven Great Sages
51. From Rocket Scientist to President Dr. APJ Abdul Kalam
52. The Visionary's Voice - Quotes of Dr. APJ Abdul Kalam
53. The Wisdom of Swami Vivekananda: Insights and Inspiration from a Legendary Spiritual Teacher
54. Ayurvedic Remedies from the Garden
55. Sages and Seers
56. Rising Strong – Motivational Stories of Women
57. Beyond Flames -Mystery stories of Funeral Ghat Manikarnika
58. The Origins of Tulsi: A Look at the Mythological Roots of the Plant"

CONTACT

DR. JAGADEESH PILLAI

MBA & PhD in Vedic Science

Four Times Guinness World Record Holder

Winner of Mahatma Gandhi Vishwa Shanti Puraskar and
Global Peace Ambassador

Gemology, Astro & Vastu Consultant - Spiritual Counselor

Consultant for designing World Record Ideas

Efficient Tarot Card Reader

9839093003

myrichindia@gmail.com

drjagadeeshpillai@facebook

drjagadeeshpillai@instagram

jagadeeshpillai@youtube

www. JAGADEESHPILLAI.com

൫

|| LOKAHA SAMASTHAHA SUKHINO BHAVANTU ||